Hand & Machine Quilting
Tips & Tricks
TOOL

- **Quilt Like the Experts**

- **Easy-To-Use Quick Reference Guide**

- **From Planning to Perfect Stitching**

Harriet Hargrave
Alex Anderson

C&T PUBLISHING

Text copyright © C&T by Publishing

Publisher: Amy Marson

Editorial Director: Gailen Runge

Acquisitions Editor: Jan Grigsby

Editor: Liz Aneloski

Technical Editors: Helen Frost and Elin Thomas

Copyeditor/Proofreader: Wordfirm Inc.

Cover Designer/Book Designer: Kristen Yenche

Production Coordinator: Matthew Allen

Photography by C&T Publishing, Inc., unless otherwise noted

Published by C&T Publishing, Inc., P.O. Box 1456, Lafayette, CA 94549

Library of Congress Cataloging-in-Publication Data

Anderson, Alex

  Hand and machine quilting tips & tricks tool : quilt like the experts, easy-to-use quick reference guide : from planning to perfect stitching / Alex Anderson, Harriet Hargrave.

     p. cm.

  ISBN-13: 978-1-57120-462-2 (paper trade : alk. paper)

  ISBN-10: 1-57120-462-8 (paper trade : alk. paper)

 1. Quilting--Patterns. 2. Patchwork--Patterns. I. Hargrave, Harriet. II. Title.

TT835.A493625 2007

746.46'041--dc22

                           2007006219

Printed in China

10 9 8 7 6 5 4 3 2

For More
Detailed Information

For further reading and more detailed information on many of the topics included in this book, please refer to these books:

AUTHOR WEBSITES:

www.harriethargrave.com

www.alexandersonquilts.com

Contents

Quick Reference
GUIDE

Alex Anderson

For more detailed information see *Hand Quilting with Alex Anderson* and *Beautifully Quilted with Alex Anderson.*

HAND QUILTING

Fabric Choices

- Always use the best 100% cotton fabric available.

- Use solid-colored or soft texture-prints that read solid to allow the quilting designs to show well.

- Avoid bed sheets and decorator fabrics for hand quilting; their higher thread count makes them difficult to hand quilt through.

Batting

- Test how easy a batting will be to hand quilt by taking a few stitches, through just the batting, with the needle you will be using (without thread).

- Purchase good-quality batting.

  Cotton batting beards less than polyester batting, looks beautiful, must be heavily quilted (every 1″ to 2″), and can be more difficult to hand quilt than polyester or wool batting.

  Polyester batting doesn't need to be quilted as heavily as cotton batting (every 2″ to 3″). Low loft gives a flat, drapey look; medium loft adds more body and provides more warmth than low loft. Don't use high loft for hand quilting.

  Cotton/polyester blend batting has the look and feel of cotton but can be almost as easy to hand quilt as polyester. Blends beard very little. They need to be quilted every 3″ or less.

  Wool batting is easy to quilt, but it's more expensive than the other types of batting.

Choosing Quilting Designs

You can find quilting design inspiration everywhere: antique quilts; quilts at quilt shows; quilting stencils, personal, public, and guild library books; and the outside world, including architecture.

Stained glass design inspiration

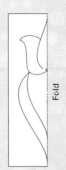

Half of tulip

Tulip

Multiple-tulip design

Porch design inspiration

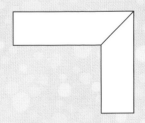

Cut the paper and mark the 45° corner.

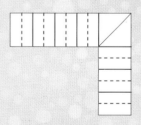

Evenly divide the space.

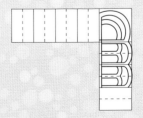

Draw multiple arcs and the corner.

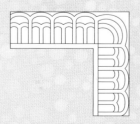

Completed design

- Fill the space.
- Use an adequate amount of quilting.
- Use an equal amount of quilting across the entire quilt surface.

Quilting over pieced units is okay; it blends the elements of the quilt top.

Uneven amount of
quilting across the surface

Adequate amount of quilting
distributed evenly across the surface

Use a quilted grid to fill an open area or to help accentuate a quilting design.

Motif without
grid quilting

Motif with
grid quilting

Sometimes just changing the thread color will make the design more prominent.

Quilting with
white thread

Quilting with
pink thread

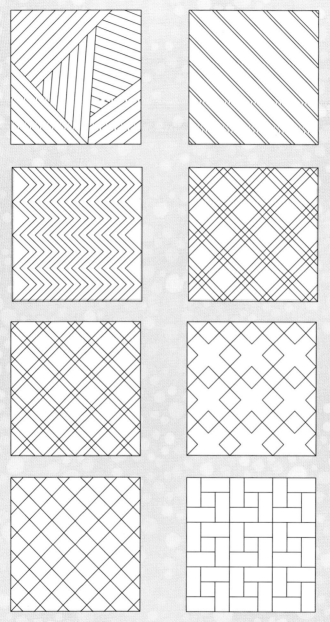

Use geometric grids on complicated quilts.

Modifying Quilting Designs

○ You can make simple changes to designs to make them your own. Trace the existing design onto paper and add or delete lines.

Original double cable design

Overlapping lines added to a double cable

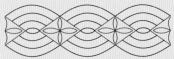

Motif added to a triple cable

Feather replacing half of a triple cable

○ Use a photocopy machine to enlarge or reduce the design to fit your space.

Making Quilting Designs

○ If you will be drawing multiple circles using a compass, reinforce the center of the paper, where the point of the compass will be, by placing a little piece of masking tape on the back.

○ It's easier to draw an arc away from your body than toward your body.

Folded-Paper Quilting Designs

Eight-Section Designs

Cut a square of paper ¼˝ smaller on all sides than the space you need to fill with quilting.

Fold in half.   Fold in half again.

Fold in half diagonally.   Draw and cut an arc.

Draw interior lines, if desired.

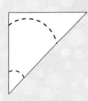

Or cut another arc at the corner of the triangle.

Then trace the cut shape onto another piece of paper and add outer scallops.

Twelve-Section Designs

Cut a square of paper ¼˝ smaller on all sides than the space you need to fill with quilting.

Fold in half.   Fold in half again.

Fold in thirds.

Draw and cut an arc.   Or cut another arc at the corner of the triangle.

Then draw interior lines, if desired.

Marking Quilting Designs

○ My favorite marking tool is a silver Verithin pencil for marking quilting designs, and I use a white charcoal pencil or white chalk powder to make additions and corrections while quilting.

○ Many great marking tools are available. Always test your marking tool to make sure the marks will come out.

○ Never use a no. 2 soft graphite pencil. The marks cannot easily be removed from fabric.

○ ¼″-wide masking tape is a great option for marking straight lines.

○ If you don't have a light table or a window with light coming through it for tracing quilting designs onto the quilt top, you can make a temporary light table by placing a lamp under

- a glass coffee table

- a piece of Plexiglas resting between two chairs

- a dining table with a piece of Plexiglas in the opening for the leaf.

○ I like to mark the entire quilt before I baste it.

○ If you will be quilting in a hoop, mark the lines darker than you would if you were working on a frame.

Basting

○ When basting a quilt, use the bowl end of a spoon to pick up the tip of the needle as it comes up through all the layers.

○ When basting a quilt, don't bother knotting the second end of the thread. When it's time to remove the basting, you can just tug on the knotted end of the thread, and it will pull out easily.

○ I baste in a 4″ grid pattern, working from the center out to the edges.

Quilting

○ When you first start hand quilting, start with a size 8 betweens needle. Work your way to the smallest needle you're comfortable with (the higher the number, the smaller the needle).

○ I like to use a size 10 betweens needle for hand quilting.

○ Traditionally, the thought was to use quilting thread with a fiber content that matched that of the quilt. However, threads have come a long way. Experiment with different threads and see what works best for you.

○ Always use good-quality thimbles. Be sure they have deep dimples and fit comfortably.

○ If you quilt with a thimble on your thumb, be sure it has good indentations on the side.

○ I recommend that you learn to quilt using a hoop and then graduate to a quilt frame if you have the space. I use a floor quilt frame my dad built.

○ When hand quilting in a hoop, work from the center of the quilt out to the edges to avoid puckers and folds in the quilt layers.

- Remove the hoop from the quilt between quilting sessions to prevent any stretching or distortion that may result from leaving the hoop on the quilt for extended periods of time.

- Don't worry about the size of your stitches. Just try for a consistent stitch length. Smaller stitches will come with practice.

- Don't pick out poor stitches as you go along. When the quilt is complete, locate those unsightly stitches and redo them; but I'm sure you'll find doing so is not worth your time.

- If your first stitch is always bigger than the rest, try inserting your needle tilted a little bit more forward than straight up and down, or consider taking a back-stitch to "cheat" the look.

- If there are several layers of fabric to quilt through (as when you go through seam allowances), consider using a stab stitch. Pass the needle through the top of the quilt to the back of the quilt, pull the needle so the thread is taut, then push the needle back up through the quilt to the top and pull the thread taut.

- If the distance between two motifs you're quilting is less than two needle lengths, consider "walking the needle" between the motifs. In the direction you want to move, insert the needle between the pieced top and the quilt backing. Push the needle halfway, so the tip of the needle is between the quilt top and backing. Bring the tip of the needle halfway up through the top of the quilt, allowing the eye to go between the quilt top and the backing. Grasp the tip of the needle and rotate the needle 180°, so that the eye (which is still between the quilt top and backing) is pointing in the direction you want to go. Push the needle through the batting in the desired direction, leading with the eye of the needle. When you get to the desired location, push the eye of the needle up through the top surface of the quilt.

Insert the needle between the layers.

Pivot the needle between the layers and push the eye of the needle through.

Correct Hand and Needle Position

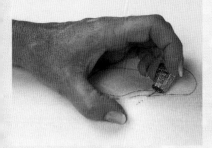

Left-handed, thimble on middle finger

Right-handed, thimble on middle finger

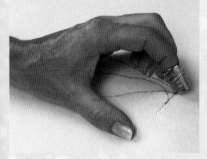

Left-handed, thimble on pointer finger

Right-handed, thimble on pointer finger

Left-handed, thimble on thumb

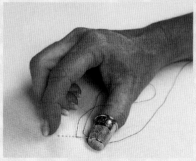

Right-handed, thimble on thumb

Batting

BATTING FIBER CONTENT

Use the rating system below to evaluate the pros and cons of each batting fiber. The ratings range from 1 to 5, with 1 representing the best performance or most expensive and 5 representing the poorest performance or least expensive.

CHARACTERISTIC	POLYESTER	COTTON	WOOL	SILK
Consistency of fiber	1	4	4	3
Washability	2	3[1]	3	3
Shrinkage	1	3	4	—[2]
Warmth (perceived)	1[3]	3	1	2
Ease of quilting	2	3[4]	1	3
Resiliency (rebound)	1–2[5]	5	1	4
Breathability	5	3	2	1
Longevity	4	1	1	3
Price	4–5	3	2	1

[1] Washability depends on the quality and type of cotton fiber used. Some cottons wash as well as or better than polyester. Also consider the quality of polyester.

[2] Information not available.

[3] Polyester is warm to some people—and very hot to others. Polyester does not breath like wool, and it holds heat next to the body. For some people, this is the only way to stay warm; for others, using a polyester-filled quilt is like being wrapped in plastic and is uncomfortable.

[4] Some cotton battings are easily quilted; others are difficult. The ease of quilting depends on the length of the fibers, as well as the bonding process used, especially if scrim has been applied.

[5] Resiliency depends on the type of fiber used. The newer, finer polyesters that are resin bonded with the soft resins now available are much easier to work.

Polyester

- Polyester battings can give you the loft that is lacking in cottons, as well as more warmth. However, some people find polyester a fairly hot product to sleep under because it does not breathe and it prevents heat and moisture from dissipating.

- Polyester battings tend to be very stretchy and are not the best choice for a quilt that is going to hang on a wall for any length of time.

- Distortion is a problem when some areas are quilted heavily and others lightly.

- Polyester is one of the most difficult battings to machine quilt, but hand quilters tend to get very small stitches in the new soft products.

- Polyester does not shrink, so an "antique" appearance is not possible, but if loft and a smooth look are what you want, it does a nice job.

From Harriet Hargrave's Quick-Look Guide: Choosing Batting

For more information see *Heirloom Machine Quilting* (4th edition)

Cotton

- Cotton sticks to the fabric, making machine quilting easy, but it can be more difficult for some hand quilters to needle. Bleaching cotton dries the fiber, causing more drag on the thread when you are hand quilting. The natural, unbleached battings tend to be easier for hand quilters to use.

- Cotton shrinks, giving an "antique" look to quilts if you don't prewash the batting and fabrics.

- Cotton is a comfortable fiber. It breathes, allowing excess heat to escape and keeping you from getting too warm. It is one of the best fibers for baby quilts.

- Cotton endures, becoming softer with age, if quilted adequately.

Wool

- Wool is very warm and lofty without being heavy. It retains its loft and recovers from compression better than any other fiber. This resiliency offers long-lasting beauty and warmth. Wool quilts and comforters can be aired twice a year to restore loft and fullness to the fiber.

- Wool breaths, keeping it from getting hot and keeping the skin warm, yet dry. It moderates temperature, so that you never get overly hot or cold sleeping under it.

- Wool can also absorb up to 33% of its own weight in moisture without feeling damp, as opposed to 4% for synthetics. This characteristic makes wool perfect for use in a damp, cold climate.

- Wool is naturally flame resistant. When it's exposed to fire, it smolders at a low temperature and self-extinguishes with a cool ash, making it an extremely safe fiber to use for small children.

- Wool is extremely easy to hand quilt.

Silk

Today's silk battings can be hand washed in cold water, drip dried, and air fluffed. Heat cannot be used at any time. Silk battings can be made thin or thick depending on how much you stretch and feather the fibers onto the project. Stitching lines should be within a 1½˝ minimum, and excess handling of the batting should be avoided.

BRAND NAME & FIBER CONTENT	QUILTING DISTANCE	USES
Mountain Mist Blue Ribbon 100% cotton	Up to 2″	Antique quilt tops and reproductions, small quilts, clothing
Quilters Dream Cotton 100% cotton (natural, white)	Up to 8″	Quilts, wallhangings, garments
Mountain Mist 100% natural cotton	¼″–1″	Antique quilt tops, antique quilt reproductions, wallhangings, baby quilts, hot pads
Warm and Natural 100% cotton	Up to 10″	Wallhangings, crafts, garments
Fairfield Soft Touch 100% cotton (bleached)	Up to 2″	Quilts, wallhangings
Hobbs Organic 100% cotton	Up to 2″	Quilts, garments
Hobbs Organic Craft Cotton 100% cotton	Up to 6″	Quilts, crafts, wallhangings
Fairfield Cotton Classic 80% cotton, 20% polyester	2″–4″	Quilts, small quilts, table cloths, placemats, garments
Hobbs Heirloom Premium Cotton 80% cotton, 20% polyester	¼″–3″	Quilts, wallhangings, baby quilts, garments
Double Brushed Cotton Flannelette 100% cotton	Any distance	Lightweight quilts, baby quilts, lap robes, summer-weight coverlets, tablecloths, placemats, garments
Quilters Dream Poly 100% polyester	Up to 8″	Quilts, wallhangings, garments
Hobbs Poly-Down Polyester 100% polyester	Up to 3″	Quilts, throws, lap quilts, pillows
Mountain Mist Glazene Process and Quilt-Light 100% polyester	Up to 2½″	Bed quilts, lap quilts
Fairfield Low Loft, Extra Loft, High Loft 100% polyester	2″–4″	Bed quilts, lap quilts, pillows, stuffing
Wool 100% wool	1″–4″	Tied comforters, quilts
Hobbs Heirloom Premium 100% wool	1″–3″	Quilts, lap quilts, throws, garments
Hobbs Thermore Thermal bonded	Up to 4″	Quilts, wallhangings, miniature quilts, garments

CHARACTERISTICS
Moderate to low shrinkage; layers stick together; cool in summer; adjusts to body temperature; breathes; cannot be preshrunk; flat, thin
Prewashing not recommended; 1% shrinkage; gives traditional look and feel to quilt; warm yet light; retains air
5%+ shrinkage; layers stick together; cool in summer, warm in winter; adjusts to body temperature; drapable; cuddly; breathes; cannot be preshrunk; gives antique appearance
Can be presoaked if desired; can be stiff if over-quilted; very flat, thin
Soft; stretches; drapes well; good stitch definition; can be preshrunk if desired
Soft drape; pliable; extremely easy to hand quilt; can be preshrunk if desired; flat, thin
Soft drape; pliable; extremely easy to hand quilt; can be preshrunk; flat, thin
Moderate to low shrinkage, shrinkage allowance should be checked; can be presoaked if desired; breathes; cool in summer; flat, thin
Can be presoaked if desired; extremely easy to hand quilt; durable; drapable; soft; warm
Can shrink to give antique appearance, no loft; high quality with adequate thread count
Do not prewash; polyester microfibers have "high wicking" properties; very drapable
Warm; very lightweight; very washable; good loft retention; extremely soft and resilient; moderately thin
Fibers shift to fill space available; can be quilted extremely close without getting stiff; does not shrink; has look and feel of cotton; heat sensitive; thin to moderately puffy
Warm; lightweight; heat sensitive; stretches and distorts if hung; low recovery from compression; does not shrink; moderate to high loft
Must be encased in cheesecloth; presoaking not recommended; high resilience; warm in cold, damp climates; puffy
Soft; drapable; can be presoaked; very warm in cold, damp climates; more comfortable than polyester; slight bearding if any; resilient; low loft
Extremely drapable; easy to quilt; lightweight; does not beard; very thin

Batting Checklist ✔

When choosing a batting for a quilt top, ask yourself the following questions:

- O Do I want the quilt to be thick or thin?

- O Do I want the quilt to look flat or fluffy?

- O Do I want to hand or machine quilt it?

- O Do I like to quilt? How close do I want to quilt this quilt?

- O Do I need this quilt for warmth, or do I want a "cooler" quilt? Is it for summer, spring, fall, or winter temperatures?

- O Is the finished quilt going to be washed a lot, or is it just for show?

- O Did I prewash my fabrics? Do I want the quilt to look antique or contemporary?

- O Is the quilt going to hang on the wall or lie on a bed?

- O Do I want a natural, synthetic, or blended fiber batting?

Harriet Hargrave

For more detailed information, see *Heirloom Machine Quilting* (4th edition).

MACHINE QUILTING
Work Space
Sewing Machine Cabinets

○ Use a sewing machine cabinet or a large extension table with a surface that is even with the bed of your machine. A large work surface will support the weight of the quilt and give your fingers room to manipulate the quilt under the needle as you're quilting.

Here are some things to keep in mind when choosing a sewing cabinet:

○ Sit in a good chair in front of the machine. Be sure that you have enough room and that you will have a good view while quilting.

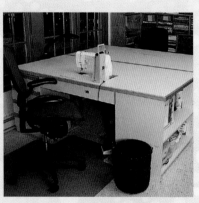

Large work surface suitable for machine quilting

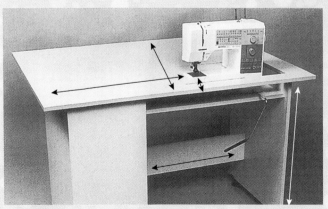

Important measurements for personalizing a machine cabinet

○ Sit at different cabinets. Your feet should be flat on the floor. Your arms should be at your sides, with elbows bent at a 100° to 110° angle (that is, hands a bit lower than elbows) and wrists resting on the cabinet top.

○ Be sure you're sitting high enough to see down the front of the machine and into the hole in the throat plate where the needle enters.

○ Be sure you can sit directly in front of the needle.

○ I like to have 3′ to 4′ to my left on the cabinet surface and 4′ to 5′ behind the machine. You can place additional tables around the cabinet to add space. (See page 23.)

○ Make sure there is a perfectly smooth transition between the sewing machine and the cabinet surfaces. Any uneven areas will interfere with the smooth movement of your hands that is necessary for even quilting.

○ The needle should be more than 6″ from the edge of the work surface, so that you can stitch with control and comfort. You should be able to rest your forearms on the edge of the cabinet and relax your hands over the fabric, and still easily see the needle entering the machine.

○ Once you've determined a comfortable setup, have an insert custom cut to accommodate the new machine position, if necessary.

Extension Tables

○ Have an extension table custom made from a smooth-surface product such as laminate-covered ¾″ particle-board countertop material. It can be as large as your table surface. Trace around the bed of your machine to make a pattern. Use this pattern to trace around and cut an opening that will fit tightly around the bed of your machine.

Chairs

○ Try out as many chairs as you can until you find the perfect one. Base your choice on comfort rather than price alone.

○ Buy the best chair you can afford. You can often find high-quality, inexpensive chairs at railroad salvage stores, used-office-equipment stores, government auctions, surplus warehouses, and on eBay.

Here are some features your chair should have:

✓ A center hydraulic-lift system to adjust the height of the chair. Your chair should be low enough so that your feet rest flat on the floor, your forearms and hands are at the proper angle to the sewing surface, and you can look down on your work as you quilt. Your thighs should be parallel to the floor (at a 90° angle to your torso), or nearly so, when you're seated. If you can't find a chair that will adjust to meet all of these requirements, give priority to the position of your arms. You can always use a platform to make up for any gap between your feet and the floor.

✓ A seat with a forward-tilt adjustment. This takes pressure off the back of your legs and keeps your back straighter.

✓ A seat that is proportional to your size.

✓ An adjustable back. Whether you sit on the edge of the chair or in the center of the seat, the chair back should adjust to reach your back and provide support.

✓ Five casters (feet) on the base to insure good balance and stability.

✓ Adjustable arms (if you prefer them) that can be moved out of the way when you don't need them.

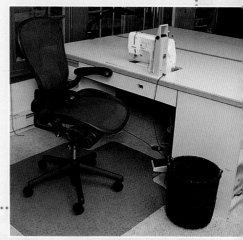

Herman Miller Aeron chair

Lighting

Lights should have enough shading to eliminate glare.

Use bulbs with adequate but not excessive wattage.

Light colors on ceilings, walls, floors, and furnishings enhance both natural and artificial light.

Avoid excessive contrast in the amounts of light in different areas of the room. More overall lighting can alleviate this problem.

Eliminate shadows. If you have a window in your work space, place your sewing machine so the natural light falls on the needle area. Use task lighting to eliminate shadows on your sewing machine needle area. Use an OTT-LITE or other nonglare, TrueColor, full-spectrum light in front of the needle, to the right, and in front of the control panel. I also place a FlexArm light behind and to the side of the machine.

◎ If the light built into your machine casts a glare off the surface of your presser foot, turn the light off to see whether your vision improves.

◎ If your room has windows and you often work at night, close the blinds when it gets dark. You can lose up to 30% of the light output in your room through windows in a dark space.

◎ Take care of your eyes; wear reading glasses when you quilt. Wearing glasses can really add visual sharpness to the area you are stitching.

◎ Every 20 minutes or so, stop the machine, look up, blink, and focus your eyes on something in the distance. If your eyes feel dry, stop and close them for a minute. Use moisturizing eye drops if needed.

OTT-LITEs surrounding
sewing machine

Layering Tables

A multipurpose table (for cutting and layering) should be customized to your body measurements, as well as to your space requirements.

Dual-purpose work surface for cutting and layering

Your table should be below elbow level and prevent you from stooping. To find your perfect table height, stand in the shoes you normally work in, bend an elbow at a 90° angle and have a friend measure from your elbow to the floor; then subtract 2″ to 3″ from this measurement.

If you use a folding banquet table, raise the table using lengths of metal or PVC pipe (choose a pipe diameter that will just slip over the table legs).

PVC leg extensions

Another option for raising a banquet table is to use 4 × 4 lumber. Cut four pieces, drill a hole the size of the table leg into the top of each piece, and then cut the pieces to the proper length.

Your table should be accessible from all four sides.

A table 28″ to 36″ wide and 56″ to 72″ long will work for layering any size quilt. The narrow width helps eliminate stress on your lower back.

Place a rubber or padded mat on the floor in front of the table to reduce circulation problems and fatigue.

Place a small footstool where you stand; alternately rest one foot and then the other on the stool. This will help keep your back straight.

Sewing Machine

Purchasing a Machine

WHAT TO LOOK FOR IN A SEWING MACHINE FOR QUILTING

✓ Perfect tension adjustment. You'll need the ability to adjust both the bobbin and the top tensions.

✓ Automatic needle stop. The needle should stop immediately rather than coasting one or two more stitches.

✓ Up-or-down needle position on command.

✓ An easily controllable foot pedal, one that is not too sensitive or too difficult.

✓ A powerful motor to prevent the machine and foot pedal from overheating during long sewing sessions.

✓ Built-in variable-speed control to control the stitching speed (optional).

✓ A clearly visible needle bar; you must be able to see the needle easily.

✓ Adjustable presser-foot pressure.

✓ High-quality feet and accessories made specifically for the machine: darning (free-motion) foot, walking foot, straight-stitch throat plate.

✓ A reputable dealer who can help with minor adjustments and who understands your technical needs.

○ Ask for a demonstration.

○ Ask to try the machine out at home over the weekend.

○ Test any machines you're interested in using your own fabric, thread, and batting samples.

Cleaning and Care

- Keep your machine covered when it's not in use.

- Keep your machine free of dust, lint, pet hair, and other foreign elements that can cause all sorts of problems, especially for the circuit boards of computerized machines.

- Follow the manufacturer's instructions for cleaning your machine.

- Use your computer's tiny vacuum attachment to remove lint and loose threads from hard-to-reach places in your sewing machine.

- Clean your machine and oil it regularly with sewing machine oil. Never use 3-IN-ONE oil or WD-40.

- When opening a container of machine oil, poke the nozzle tip with a pin so that the oil comes out in tiny drops.

- After oiling, rethread the machine and stitch on a fabric scrap until there is no oil on the thread.

Sewing Machine Accessories

- If you are machine quilting with the feed dogs up, use a walking or even-feet foot so that the layers of the quilt move evenly under the presser foot. There should be no shifting or pushing of the layers.

Variety of walking feet

- Use a walking foot with a guide bar to aid in stitching parallel lines.

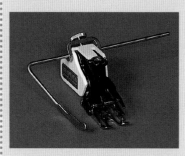

Walking foot with guide bar

O If your walking foot has trouble passing over multiple layers and seam allowances, you can remove the short center feeder, which is located in the center directly behind the needle, with a utility knife or small power grinder.

O A walking foot with an open toe allows you to clearly see what you are quilting. If you don't have an open-toe walking foot, you can modify your walking foot as follows:

Use a small power grinder to cut through the metal to make a wider opening (open toe).

Walking foot before and after opening the toe

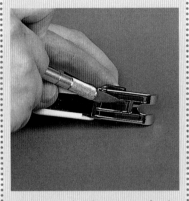

Cutting out the short center feeder

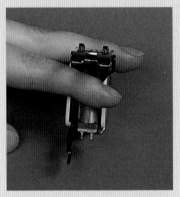

Channel created by removing the center feeder

○ If your machine has the capability, adjust the presser-foot pressure to put just the right amount of pressure on the quilt layers so that they feed smoothly.

○ Use a darning foot with the feed dogs down or covered for free-motion quilting.

○ Use a small, round, closed-toe foot that measures ¼″ or smaller from the needle to each edge of the foot for most free-motion machine quilting.

○ For most free-motion quilting, an open-toe darning foot is problematic. The toe gets caught in the threads and tends to push bits of fabric in front of the toe, which leads to the formation of tucks.

¼″ closed- and open-toe darning feet

○ An open-toe foot is helpful for quilting very small areas and for stitching tiny echo lines or stippling.

○ Large quilting feet work best for quilting thick quilts, such as those made with flannel, wool, or high-loft polyester batting.

Large quilting feet

○ When you are quilting a trapunto design, use a larger quilting foot to accommodate the added thickness of the second layer of batting.

○ Some larger feet do not sit close enough to the fabric to prevent skipped stitches when you are using a thin batting. If skipped stitches are a problem, try a different foot to see whether the clearances are causing the problem.

- ○ Try to collect all three free-motion feet (open-toe foot, closed-toe foot, and large quilting foot). Practice with each of them in different situations to see when each works best for you.

- ○ Try using a straight-stitch (single-hole) throat plate. It can prevent problems with poor stitch quality.

Zigzag and straight-stitch (single-hole) throat plates

- ○ If you are experiencing cuts or thread snags, make sure the hole in the throat plate doesn't have any burrs or chips on it.

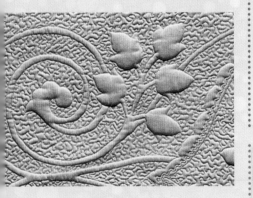

Threads

- ○ Consider your quilting skills when choosing fabrics. Stitching shows on solid-colored fabrics and is hidden on busy prints.

Stitching on solid-colored fabric

- ○ Use only high-quality thread. It is soft, strong, smooth, and lustrous, and it resists shrinkage. It should have long staple fibers (no slubs or fuzzy appearance).

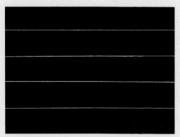

**Top: High-quality thread.
Bottom three: Slubs and fuzziness.**

- ○ Use natural-fiber (cotton or silk) thread on quilts made of natural fibers and synthetic thread on quilts made of synthetic fabrics. The exception is nylon monofilament thread, which works well on quilts of any fiber content.

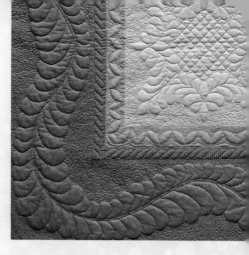

○ Thread sizes are usually referred to using the English sizing system. There is often an "Ne" in front of the numbers (50/3 or 60/2). But some thread companies (YLI, Superior, Signature) use the American sizing system (Tex). If you use a Tex system thread, the number does not mean the same thing as the number on commonly available Ne threads, and the ply is not always indicated.

○ I recommend high-quality 50-weight three-ply mercerized cotton thread for quilting medium-weight cotton quilting fabrics.

Variety of 50/3 sewing threads

○ Try various types and weights of threads to see whether they are right for the look you prefer, and for your machine.

Nylon Thread

Note: Be extremely careful about which nylon thread you select. I have been using nylon for more than 28 years and have had no problems with broken stitches and damaged fabric, even though my quilts are washed six to eight times a year, travel constantly, and are exposed monthly to severe heat and cold in airplanes. I feel that nylon thread has been grossly maligned and that it offers many more positives than negatives for machine quilting.

○ Nylon thread is a good choice for beginning machine quilters. It is very forgiving and encourages the beginner to keep quilting, because mistakes and uneven stitches are nearly invisible.

○ Use only the finest, highest-quality nylon threads. I suggest Sew-Art International Invisible Nylon thread (it's not shiny and is my preference) and YLI Wonder Invisible Thread. Use .004-weight nylon on cardboard tubes or small white cones. Heavier nylon thread can tear the fabric and break the bobbin thread.

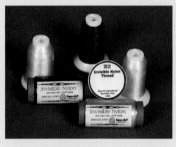

Tubes and cones of .004-weight Invisible Nylon thread

○ Nylon thread should be smooth and as fine as a hair.

○ As you approach the end of a spool of nylon, the thread often begins to feel rough, take on the shape of the spool, and start to coil. When this happens, throw the spool away and replace it with a fresh one.

○ Use cotton thread in the bobbin when using nylon thread. NEVER use polyester thread in the bobbin; the abrasive poly-ester fibers will serrate the nylon, causing broken stitches.

○ When using cotton thread in the bobbin, match the color to the color of the backing fabric.

○ You can use nylon thread in the bobbin, but it tends to leave a stiff, harsh line of stitching rather than the soft, up-and-down look of cotton and nylon used together. Using nylon on the top and bobbin also lends itself to snarling and breaking threads.

○ The only time I use nylon in the bobbin is when I quilt back-to-front using the backing print as the quilting design, because the bobbin thread ends up on the front of the quilt. I use cotton as the top thread.

○ When winding nylon thread onto the bobbin, use your fingers to guide the thread onto the bobbin as you run the machine. Do not use the thread guides and tension regulators; they will stretch the thread.

○ When using nylon thread, keep the stitches small; they will have built-in stretchability.

○ When using nylon thread, you will likely need to loosen your machine's top tension.

Sewing Machine Set-Up For Nylon Thread

When sewing with nylon thread that comes on the small white cone, set the cone upright on the table, on the right side, at the back of the machine.

When using nylon that comes on a spool, use a cone holder or small jar to hold the spool upright and off the machine, rather than using the spool pin on your machine. If the spool rod on the cone holder is too tall, put a small spool on the rod first and then put the spool of nylon on top of it. This arrangement prevents the nylon from wrapping around the rod. The guide at the top of the cone holder is normally bent at 45°. Use a pair of pliers to bend the rod and close the opening. Bending the rod keeps the nylon from falling off the end of the guide. Place the thread holder on the table, on the right side, at the back of the machine.

Tape a closed safety pin or pins, as shown, to guide the thread at the same angle as the spool pins.

Safety-pin thread guides (a and b)

Use pin b even if your machine has built-in thread guides.

To prevent the nylon thread from coming off the spool in snarls and loops, put a "sock" over the spool. The sock is made from a 3″ to 4″ length of $7/8''$ Surgitube Tubular Gauze (available at pharmacies).

Cone holders and jar for holding nylon when sewing

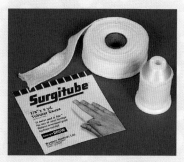

Surgitube gauze "sock"

Sewing Machine Needles

- Use only high-quality needles.

- If you are experiencing stitch problems, first change your machine needle.

- Always start each project with a new needle.

- Label a tomato pincushion for used-needle storage. Mark a different needle size and type in each section.

Labeled tomato pincushion

✓ There is a 10% imperfection rate per package of new sewing machine needles. So even a new needle may cause stitch problems.

✓ Use the needle type, size, and brand recommended for your machine and use a needle that complements your choice of thread.

NEEDLE FEATURES AND USES		
Needle Type	Features	Uses
Universal	Standard machine needle	Woven fabrics and knits
Schmetz Microtex/Sharp	Slim, sharp point	Fine, tightly-woven polyesters and microfibers
Schmetz Quilting (H–Q)	Thin, tapered, deep point	Piecing and quilting
Schmetz Embroidery (H–E)	Deep thread groove, large eye	Rayon threads
Sullivan Metafil or Schmetz Metallica (130/MET)	Double-sized eye, Teflon-coated	Metallic threads
Denim (H–J)	Stiff shaft, sharp point, slender eye	Tightly woven fabrics

SKILL LEVEL FOR NEEDLE AND THREAD USE			
Skill Level	Needle	Top Thread	Bobbin Thread
Level 1	80/12 universal (H) or sharp-point (H–M)	50/3 cotton or nylon	50/3 cotton or nylon
Level 2	75/11 universal (H) or quilting (H–Q)	50/3 cotton or nylon	50/3 cotton or nylon
Level 3	70/10 universal (H)	50/2 or 60/2 machine embroidery thread, nylon	50/2 or 60/2 machine embroidery thread or nylon
Level 4	70/10 sharp point (H–M)	50/2 or 60/2 machine embroidery thread or nylon	50/2 or 60/2 machine embroidery thread
Level 5	65/9	50/2 or 60/2 machine embroidery thread, nylon	50/2 or 60/2 machine embroidery thread or nylon
Level 6	60/8	Nylon, 50/2 or 60/2 machine embroidery thread, or 100-weight silk	Nylon, or 50/2 or 60/2 embroidery cotton

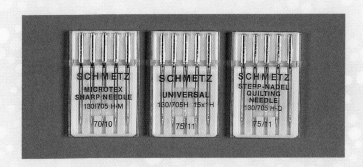

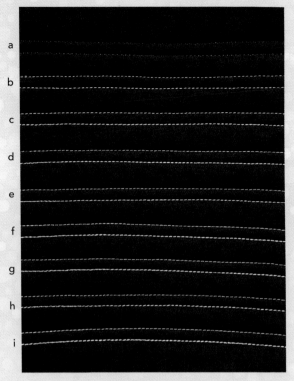

Single and double-stitched lines:

(a) Sew-Art .004-weight Invisible Nylon,
(b) YLI 100 silk,
(c) Tire 50 silk,
(d) Mettler 60/2 embroidery cotton,
(e) DMC 50/2 embroidery cotton,
(f) Mettler 30/2 embroidery cotton,
(g) Mettler 50/3 cotton,
(h) YLI Machine Quilting thread 40 TEX,
(i) Mettler 40/3 quilting thread

⊙ Use a large needle and heavy thread for quilting patterns with large spaces between the lines. Use a fine needle and very fine thread for tiny stippling, echo quilting, or very small shapes.

⊙ Use a 70/10 or smaller needle for ditch quilting to ensure that the stitching is right in the ditch.

Planning Ahead

- ○ Consider the machine quilting process before constructing the quilt top. A little preplanning will prevent tucks, puckers, stretching, and distortion when you quilt and will give you beautiful results.

Fabric Choices

- ○ Consider the level of your quilting skills when choosing fabrics.

- ○ Solid and light-colored fabrics, especially muslin and whites, creams, and pastels, allow the quilting stitches to be visible and will showcase beautiful stitching.

- ○ Busy prints and dark colors allow the stitches to disappear into the fabric and don't show clearly.

Stitches show on solid fabrics, hide on prints.

Quilting Designs

- ○ Test your machine on a sample quilt sandwich of the fabric and batting you plan to use. Check the tension and stitch length.

- ○ Consider the quilting before piecing the quilt top. Plan the piecing, open spaces, sashing, and borders on the basis of specific quilting designs.

- ✓ Is the quilt traditional, contemporary, or a repro-duction? Is it a specific style—bargello, watercolor, Baltimore Album, or Amish? Choose compatible quilting designs.

- ✓ Will the quilt be purely decorative, or will it be used and laundered often?

- ✓ Do you want elaborate or simple quilting? How much time do you want to spend on quilting?

- ✓ Is the top made from busy prints that will hide the quilting, or will the quilting show up well?

- ✓ What batting will you use? According to the manufac-turer's instructions, what is the maximum distance you can have between lines of quilting?

- ✓ What are your technical skills?

- If you want to quilt intricate designs, choose light-colored fabrics that allow the marked lines to show clearly.

Thread Color

- If you want your stitches to be visible and decorative, use a heavy or contrasting-colored thread.

- If you want to disguise imperfections, use a thread that matches or totally blends into the fabric—or use nylon thread.

- Use nylon thread if the quilting lines will cross over different fabrics and colors.

Fabric Preparation

Start thinking about the finished look you want for your quilt before you do anything to your fabric.

- Experiment with samples, trying different techniques, needles, threads, and fabrics (prewashed and not prewashed) to get the look you want.

- Using prewashed fabric gives a smoother, finished look, whereas using unwashed fabric gives a slightly puckered, antique-quilt look.

- Firm fabrics—piece better and quilt better. Use starch (liquid concentrate, spray, or powder mixed with water in a spray bottle) for both prewashed and unwashed fabrics to make them flat and crisp.

Pressing Seam Allowances

- If you are planning to ditch quilt, press the seam allowances to one side.

- If you are making a block with many seams that cross, and you don't plan to ditch quilt any of the seams within the block, press the seams open to eliminate bulk at the intersections.

- Open seams make a smoother and flatter quilt top, so quilting over the seams is much easier for the machine.

- Sew, set the seam, press, lightly starch, and press again. This process will make the quilt top more secure, making it easier to mark and quilt.

Preparing Borders

- O Cut border strips wider than the desired finished width and starch them before and after attaching them to the quilt top.

- O Mark the finished width on each border with a washable marker, so you know where to stop the marked design.

- O After quilting, trim the borders to the desired finished width.

Preparing the Quilt for Marking

- O Press the quilt top well.

Stencils and Block Quilting Designs

Mark registration lines on the quilt top and the quilting design for accurate design placement.

Registration lines for quilt block

Registration lines for quilting design

Borders and Corners

1. Mark 45° angle and corner lines.

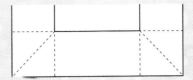

Mark 45° angle and corner lines.

2. Measure from the border seam to the edge of the border, minus ¼″ for outside edge seam allowance, and determine the midpoint of the border width. Measure out from the border seam and mark a dot at each corner on the previously drawn lines. Connect the midpoint dots with a line running the length of each border.

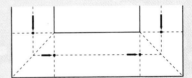

Find border width midpoints.

3. Measure the length of each border and mark the midpoint.

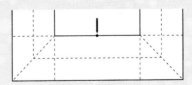

Measure the border length and mark the midpoint.

4. Draw matching 45° angle lines and border width center lines on the border stencil or design.

Paper Folding to Fit Borders (No Math)

1. Cut a strip of paper the same length as the sides of the quilt.

2. Measure the repeat of the quilting design.

3. Divide the border length by this measurement to find the number of repeats. Round up or down to the nearest number of whole repeats.

4. Fold the paper into the number of repeats from Step 3.

5. Lengthen of shorten the design repeat to fit into each folded section.

6. Draw the adjusted repeat onto the paper for the complete border length.

7. Transfer the quilting lines to the quilt. Repeat for the top and bottom borders.

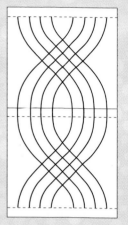

Using a paper pattern to divide distances

Preparing Border Stencils

Mark registration lines directly onto the stencil with a permanent pen.

1. Draw a 45° line for the corner.

2. Draw a line, through the center of the design, the length of the stencil.

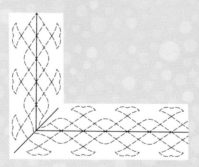

Registration lines on border stencil

3. Draw registration lines on the quilt (page 41).

4. Align the registration lines on the stencil with the registration lines on the quilt.

5. Mark the quilting lines on the quilt.

Marking Tools

- Never use a no. 2 soft graphite pencil. The marks may be permanent.

- Do not use white dressmaker's chalk. It has a high wax content, and the marks may be permanent.

- Test all marking tools before marking the quilt top to be sure the marks can be removed.

- To help keep markers from drying out, store them in resealable bags when not in use.

- Work with several of the same type of pen at a time. I use one pen until the lines just begin to get pale, and then I replace the cap tightly, store the pen cap down, and move to another pen. The resting period recharges the pen, and it lasts much longer.

- Be careful with purple air-erasable pens. Even after the color disappears, one of the chemicals remains in the fabric and causes permanent and unsightly damage if the marks are not removed thoroughly.

Marking Techniques

- Machine quilting requires bold, easy-to-see and easy-to-remove lines.

- Maintain an easy-to-mark finish by not prewashing your fabrics; or starch the fabrics to create a finish before you mark the quilt top. Then mark bold lines with a light touch. They'll be easier to remove later.

- Spray a marked area with hair spray to keep chalk marks in place for longer periods of time.

- Always clean the edges of any straight edges or rulers before using them to mark a quilt top. Ink from previous projects can leave permanent marks on your quilt.

- Try to do all the marking on the quilt top before putting the layers together, unless you are working with flannel and pounce powder or with fusible battings.

- If your quilt top slides around while you're marking it, center and secure the backing onto a table or the floor and then place your quilt top on top of the backing. The quilt top will cling to the backing, which will prevent it from slipping.

Tulle (very fine netting) or mesh are great options for marking.

1. Trace the quilting design onto tulle or mesh.

2. Position and pin the traced design on the quilt top and mark with a liquid fabric marker.

Use a wash-away (Sulky Solvy) or tear-away product (Quilt & Tear on a Roll).

Mark the quilting design on the product. Then position the product over the quilt top when layering and basting. Stitch through the paper on the design lines and then remove the product.

Using a lightbox is another great option.

Remove the sewing machine from the cabinet, place a fluorescent light where the machine usually sits, and place a thick piece of Plexiglas over the opening.

Or, make a light table.

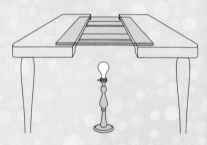

Pull the table apart, cover the opening with glass or Plexiglas, and then place a lamp (without the shade) under the table. Higher-wattage bulbs make tracing easier.

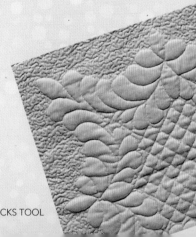

Use craft or freezer paper.

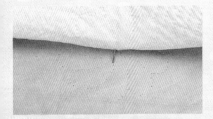

Place brown craft paper or freezer paper over a piece of cardboard, a sheet of cork, or carpeting. Place the quilt on top of the paper and then pierce holes through the quilt into the paper along the quilting lines to create a quilting design pattern. Use pounching powder to mark the design onto the quilt.

○ To use a lightbox to trace designs onto your quilt top, tape the paper pattern onto the lightbox and position the quilt top over it. You can also secure the quilt top to the lightbox to prevent slipping.

○ Do not iron or expose your marked quilt top to high heat. It can permanently set your marks.

○ To remove ink marks, completely submerge the quilt in cold water. Do not use soaps or detergents, because the sodium content can set the marks permanently. Soak the quilt until all the marks completely disappear; then launder the quilt in cool water with a neutral detergent such as Orvus Paste or Ivory to remove the chemical from the fibers.

Layering

○ The backing and batting should be the same size—2˝ to 4˝ larger than the quilt top.

○ Starch the backing fabric and layer and baste on a table to eliminate distortion and tucks on the backing.

○ Secure the backing to the table using clamps or tape.

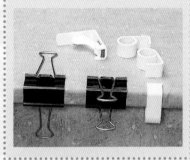

Backing taut and clamped to table

Smaller backing taped and clamped to table

O To remove the fold lines and distortion from polyester batting, place it in the clothes dryer on the lowest heat setting with a damp hand towel and tumble for 10 to 15 minutes.

O To remove the fold lines from natural-fiber batting, iron the batting using steam.

O Remove all stray threads from the back of the quilt top before layering, so they won't show through on the finished quilt.

O To remove stray threads from the back of the quilt top, use a square of cotton batting to blot them up. This method is easier than picking them off one by one!

Pin Basting

O Use pin basting rather than thread basting for machine quilting. Thread basting doesn't hold up well, and the threads get caught in the sewing machine foot as you quilt.

O Use only rustproof pins.

O I like to use size no. 1 nickel-plated or rustproof safety pins.

O Keep a velvet emery strawberry in your pin box. The abrasive emery powder is perfect for sharpening and smoothing problem pins. Squeeze the strawberry tight, push the pin in and out a few times, and then twist it several times. If this doesn't work, throw away the bad pin.

O Plastic safety-pin grip covers on your pins give your fingers more grip with less pressure and make the pins easier and more comfortable to manipulate.

Basting tools: Safety pins (with and without plastic covers), emery strawberry, Kwik Klip, and pliers.

O A Kwik Klip can help close the safety pins.

Use a Kwik Klip to close safety pins.

- Space pins 2˝ to 3˝ apart on thin cotton batting and 1˝ to 3˝ apart on wiry polyester or wool batting.

- Start pinning in the center of the quilt and work out to the edges. Avoid pinning across seam lines that will be ditch quilted or across design lines.

- Close the safety pins as you go.

Preparing for Quilting

- Roll the right-hand side of the quilt as tightly as possible, to within 2˝ of the center, to fit under the machine arm.

- Choose one of the many styles of clips to hold the rolled side of the quilt in place.

Clips for holding the rolled side of the quilt

- Place the clips down the length of the quilt. You can unroll the quilt to the right for each successive quilting line from inside the clips; you don't need to remove them each time.

Rolling the quilt to go through the machine

- Another option is to gather the bulk and spread it on the table or fold it into loose accordion pleats, instead of keeping it in a tight roll.

Thread Tension

- Always test your stitching on a sample using the fabric, batting, and thread you will be using.

- Double check your tension every time you change the stitch length on your machine.

- Thread your machine following the manufacturer's instructions to ensure perfect stitches.

- Make sure the presser-foot lever is down before you start machine stitching. It's easy to forget to do this when using a darning foot because it doesn't sit on the fabric when it's lowered. The tension is not engaged unless the presser foot is down.

Balanced tension

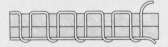

Top tension too loose or bobbin tension too tight

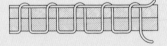

Top tension too tight or bobbin tension too loose

- If the tension is off, always adjust the top tension first. Adjust the bobbin tension only if the top tension adjustment doesn't work.

- The tension adjustments necessary for quilting can be different than those for sewing.

Bobbin Tension

- Use only bobbins made for your model and brand of machine.

- Make sure your bobbin is wound smoothly.

1 and 2. Improperly wound bobbins.
3. Properly wound bobbin.

- Thread the filled bobbin into the bobbin case. Be sure the bobbin rotates in the direction recommended by your machine manufacturer.

To test bobbin tension:

Hold the bobbin case as shown. It should not slide down under its own weight, but when you jerk your hand lightly upward, yo-yo style, the case should gently fall. If it doesn't move, the tension may be too tight. If the bobbin falls easily, the tension is probably too loose.

1. Before you adjust the bobbin tension, draw a clock as shown below. Hold the bobbin case exactly as shown and make a line on your drawing to indicate the position of the tension screw.

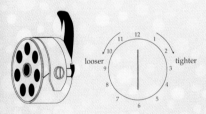

Mark a line on the clock drawing to indicate the tension screw position.

2. Turn the tension screw slightly (one-hour increments), clockwise to tighten, counterclockwise to loosen. Test after each adjustment until the tension is balanced.

3. Make another mark on your clock drawing and make a note as to which way you turned the screw. After finishing your project, refer to your note and return the screw to its original position.

○ As an alternative, you can purchase another bobbin case for these situations, leaving the original bobbin case set for normal sewing.

○ Refer to your machine dealer or mechanic or to the manufacturer's instructions if you have a drop-in bobbin housing mechanism.

○ If the tension acts up during sewing, stop, clean the machine, change the needle, and adjust the tensions again, if necessary.

○ If your machine has a difficult time sewing with nylon thread, ask your mechanic about making a slight adjustment in the machine's timing to accommodate the ultra fineness of nylon.

○ Fold a piece of fabric in half. Stitch a line of stitches on the bias using one thread color in the bobbin and another in the needle. With your hands about 3″ apart, grasp the line of stitching and pull with an even, quick snap, until one thread breaks. If the broken thread is the color of the top thread, the upper tension is too tight. If the broken thread is from the bobbin, the upper tension is too loose. If the threads break at the same time, the tension is balanced.

Stitching

I don't want to turn the quilt under the machine and I don't want more than half of the quilt under the machine at any time. Therefore, I begin stitching on the center seamline or center row of blocks and work out to the edges.

Below are some options for dealing with the bulk while sewing:

Quilt held in lap, bunched up to feed into the machine

Table on the left to support the quilt under the arm

Over-the-shoulder position

Quilt under the arm and falling to the floor, supported on the chest

Anchor Stitching

Whenever possible, quilt your quilt in-the-ditch with invisible nylon (or water-soluble thread if it will be removed later) to stabilize the layers before adding the more-detailed quilting. Use a walking foot.

1. Begin by stitching the anchoring lines.

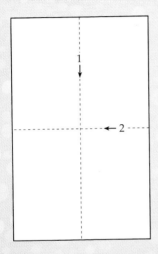

Anchoring lines for straight-set quilt

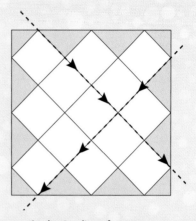

Anchoring lines for square diagonal-set quilt with offset seams

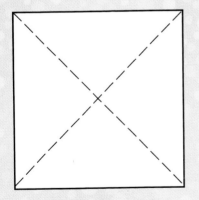

Anchoring lines for square diagonal-set quilt with seams that run from corner to corner

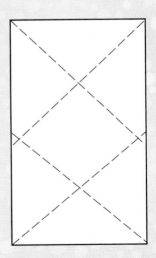

Anchoring lines for rectangular diagonal-set quilt with seams that run from corner to corner

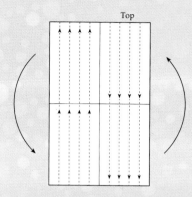

Stitch each line to the right of the center. Turn the quilt end-to-end and stitch the opposite side.

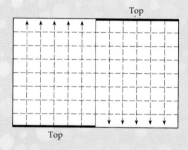

Stitch cross seams.

2. Quilt the seams that attach the borders at the same time as the lengthwise and crosswise seams; then you don't have to make a turn at the corners later.

3. Stitch diagonal seams last.

Stitching Order

Analyze your quilt top to determine what quilting elements will be included.

Pieced Quilts:

1. Anchor stitch (pages 51–52).

2. Complete other quilting that requires the walking foot.

3. Free-motion quilt all the designs within blocks and sashing strips.

4. Quilt any continuous curves in pieced blocks.

5. Stitch any grid or echo quilting in the background of blocks.

6. Stipple quilt any background areas.

7. Quilt the borders.

Appliqué Quilts:

1. Anchor stitch (pages 51–52).

2. Use the darning foot to ditch quilt around each element of every appliqué.

3. Grid, stipple, or echo quilt any background area around the appliqués.

4. Quilt the borders.

Borders:

1a. All straight lines, especially on the diagonal: Start in the center of one border and work in one direction to the corner on the right. Return to the center and quilt the lines to the left.

1b. Grid: Quilt the intersecting grid lines after the entire length has been quilted in one direction.

2. If the border includes a cable or other motif, quilt the design first and then add background stitching such as grid work or echo quilting.

3. Stipple the background area, if desired.

Quilting Techniques

Ditch Quilting

○ Use ditch quilting to stabilize the quilt, remove the basting pins you no longer need, and then finish the quilting.

○ Use ditch quilting exclusively if your quilt is made with printed fabrics than won't allow more intricate quilting to show.

○ Consider free-motion ditch quilting. With free-motion, there is no chance of distortion because the feed dogs are down, and you don't have to turn the quilt. This is a wonderful option for ditch quilting around appliquéd and pieced shapes.

○ You can make ditch quilting temporary by using water-soluble thread. This is a great option if you plan to quilt extensive diagonal grid work—it prevents distortion.

○ Use a walking foot to make stitching easy.

○ Plan the ditch quilting so only half of the bulk is under the machine at any time.

○ Press the seams well, so that they remain in position for the walking foot to feed evenly and so that the needle can come close to the ditch for the stitches to remain invisible.

○ Stitch on the side of the seam that has the single thickness of fabric. The needle should actually rub on the edge of the seam as you stitch. When the fabric relaxes, the stitching will be completely hidden in the seam.

Needle in-the-ditch on the low side of the seam, rubbing the fold on the seam allowance

○ Use a small needle (60/8 or 65/9) and nylon thread for the most invisible stitching.

Small needle with nylon thread

Large needle with nylon thread

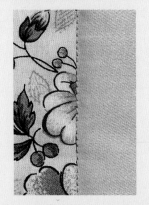

Large needle with cotton thread

○ Piece accurately and press carefully to insure straight ditch quilting.

A perfectly butted seam will give you a straight line to quilt.

○ If your intersections are off, stitch to the intersection, take two or three stitches in the same hole, lift the needle and the presser foot, move the quilt just enough to place the needle in the correct position, and then continue stitching.

The intersection is off, so you'll have to side-step when you ditch quilt.

○ If you are using a Pfaff machine with the built-in dual feed, use the open-toe appliqué foot to give yourself unobstructed vision.

1. Begin by stitching the center seam that runs with the lengthwise grain of the backing. If there is a border or sashing strip at the edge of the quilt, begin the stitching inside the border or sashing at the seamline.

2. Place your hands as shown to gently push any fullness of the top layer only back toward the foot. As you stitch, allow the excess fabric to be pulled gently into the walking foot.

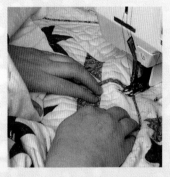

Correct hand placement, using the fingers to feed the top layer into the walking foot

3. Watch the needle as it stitches to be sure that it is rubbing the seam at every stitch along the way. Adjust your chair, if necessary.

4. At the beginning and last $1/4"$ of each line of stitching, decrease the stitch length to $1/2$ or 0.5. Stitch with these very tiny stitches (50 stitches to the inch) to lock off the stitching.

5. Each time you lock off, cut the top thread as close to the fabric as possible. When you're finished quilting, remove the quilt from the machine, turn it over and clip the bobbin threads on the back. Tug lightly on the bobbin thread to pull any top tail through the layers. Clip the bobbin thread as close as possible to the fabric.

Channel and Grid Quilting

Channel quilting outside design

Grid quilting inside and outside design

○ Use channel or grid quilting around complex quilting or appliquéd designs.

Grids can be horizontal and vertical, diagonal, double diagonal, hanging diamonds, plaids, or any combination you choose.

Variety of background grid quilting patterns

○ Carefully mark the quilting lines on the quilt top and use a walking foot for accurate, straight lines.

○ Or choose from a wide variety of precut grid and diamond stencils in various sizes available.

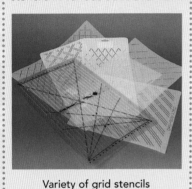

Variety of grid stencils

To mark a horizontal and vertical grid with a ruler:

1. Measure the finished sides of the block or quilt to be grid quilted.

2. Choose a grid size that is evenly divisible into the measurement.

3. Mark dots along the edges of the area to be grid quilted.

4. Connect the dots to mark the grid.

To mark a 45° grid with a ruler:

1. Measure the finished sides of the block or quilt to be grid quilted.

2. Choose an interval between dots (see chart below) that is divisible into the measurement. This interval will determine the grid size.

3. Mark dots along the edges of the area to be grid quilted.

4. Connect the dots to mark the grid.

45° DIAGONAL GRID SPACING	
Desired Grid Size	Interval Between Dots
⅜˝	½˝
½˝	¾˝
¾˝	1˝
⅞˝	1¼˝
1+˝	1½˝

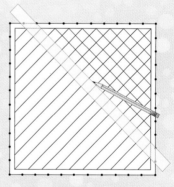

Marking and connecting dots

Another option is to use a walking foot with a guide bar. Determine the distance you want between grid lines and set the guide bar to that measurement.

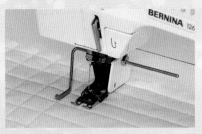

Walking foot with guide bar

If you plan to use a guide bar, note that stiffly starched fabric feeds under the walking foot easily.

When stitching triple lines, stitch the center line of all the sets first, then go back and stitch on each side.

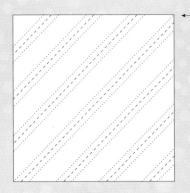

Triple-line grid

Free-Motion Quilting

- Practice, practice, practice.

- Preparation is the key to success. Choose a suitable work space and good equipment and understand your machine, needles, and thread.

- Starched fabrics will move through the machine more accurately and easily.

- Use a darning foot and a straight-stitch throat plate and drop or cover the feed dogs.

- Use the smallest darning foot available, so it doesn't obstruct your view.

- A round (rather than oval) darning foot will enable you to use its edge as a guide.

- Quilting barefoot will allow you to have much more control of the machine speed. You can feel changes of pressure more easily.

○ Always bring the bobbin thread to the top of the quilt to prevent the threads from jamming and snarling on the underside of the quilt.

○ Keep the machine speed steady. Relax and breathe.

○ If you find it too hard to keep a constant speed with your foot pedal, place a little block of wood on the back of the pedal to prevent the machine from going any faster.

○ Another option is to try one of your machine's built-in motor speeds. After you master this, try again to control the speed with your foot instead of using the machine's built-in feature.

○ Match the size of your free-motion stitches with any stitches made using the walking foot, on the same quilt. Note however that stipple quilting will sometimes look better with small stitches.

○ Rest your arms on the edge of the table or on the quilt to remove tension from your shouders and back. A good chair and good posture are critical.

○ Don't look in the hole of the foot or at the needle. Look ahead and anticipate where you're going.

○ At the beginning and last $\frac{1}{8}$" to $\frac{1}{4}$" of each line of stitching, make very tiny stitches to lock off the stitching.

○ Each time you lock off, cut the top thread as close to the fabric as possible. When you're finished quilting, remove the quilt from the machine, turn it over, and clip the bobbin threads on the back.

○ Tug lightly on the bobbin thread to pull any top tail through the layers. Clip the bobbin thread as close as possible to the fabric.

○ Adjust the quilting speed depending on the complexity, size, and shape of the design you're quilting, as well as the size of the quilt.

TROUBLESHOOTING COMMON PROBLEMS

Machine Needles Break

Cause	Solution
Quilt is moving too fast for speed of needle	maintain appropriate and consistent machine speed and smooth, even hand movements.
Top thread may be wrapped around something, preventing it from feeding smoothly	check to be sure thread is unobstructed.
Needle is too small	try a larger needle.

Uneven Stitches

Cause	Solution
Machine bed is sticky	clean with rubbing alcohol, and then wax and buff.
Prewashed fabric is dragging against the machine	starch the fabric.
Machine speed or hand speed is erratic	maintain consistent machine speed and smooth, even hand movements.
You may be sitting too low for proper eye-hand coordination	raise your chair.
Your machine is too far away for you to have steady control	adjust distance.
Your fingers have no grip on the fabric, so you're pressing down on it to move it, which creates more resistance	use file fingers or gloves to improve your grip.
Your darning foot rides too low on the quilt	reduce the presser foot tension or use the large quilting foot on your machine.
Your mind is wandering	take a break.

Other books from Alex

Other books from
Harriet

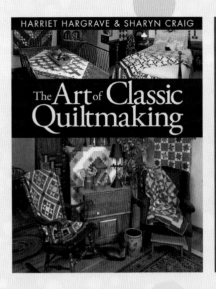

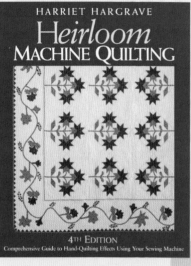

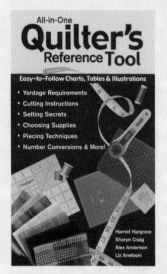

The Machine Quilting Classic
in its 4th Edition!

This newly updated classic includes everything you need to know about straight-line and free-motion quilting, elegant feathers, and padded quilting.

- In-depth instruction for every step from planning and preparation to detailed quilting techniques

- Includes new techniques and tips developed since the 3rd edition

- Updated in full color, including 4 quilt galleries that highlight quilting details

"A fabulous resource for quiltmakers interested in beginning or mastering machine quilting. Spiral bound for easy use."

—Quiltmaker

"This book has become my quilting bible."

—Reader review

"If you are just thinking of trying machine quilting or you are a long time fan, you will want to add this to your quilting library"

—The Appliqué Society

HARRIET HARGRAVE
Heirloom
MACHINE QUILTING

4TH EDITION
Comprehensive Guide to Hand-Quilting Effects Using Your Sewing Machine

$29.95, #10346, 176p, color, spiral bound. Available in Spanish.

ISBN 1-57120-236-6, UPC 734817-103462

Other
Great Products
From C&T

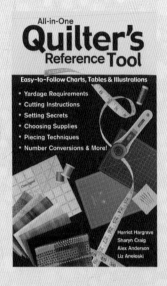